Passengers Once More
New and reopened stations
and lines since 1948

SOUTHERN ENGLAND
Greater London
and Essex to Gloucestershire

Electric unit No 319219 leaves West Brompton on a Brighton to Watford Junction service on 28 July 2004

Passengers Once More
New and reopened stations and lines since 1948

SOUTHERN ENGLAND
Greater London
and Essex to Gloucestershire
Terry Gough ARPS

Silver Link Publishing Ltd

First published in 2011

British Library Cataloguing in Publication Data

A catalogue record for this book is available from the British Library.

ISBN 978 1 85895 356 6

Silver Link Publishing Ltd
The Trundle
Ringstead Road
Great Addington
Kettering
Northants NN14 4BW

Tel/Fax: 01536 330588
email: sales@nostalgiacollection.com
Website: www.nostalgiacollection.com

Printed and bound in the Czech Republic

Abbreviations

ALCRP	Abbey Line Community Rail Partnership		**LSWR**	London & South Western Railway
AVR	Avon Valley Railway		**LUL**	London Underground Limited
BR(E)	British Railways, Eastern Region		**Met**	Metropolitan Railway
BR(W)	British Railways, Western Region		**Met-Dist**	Metropolitan District Railway
BR(S)	British Railways, Southern Region		**MR**	Midland Railway
CR	Chiltern Railways		**MSWJR**	Midland & South Western Junction Railway
c2c	c2c Rail Ltd (part of National Express)		**MVCRP**	Marston Vale Community Rail Partnership
CWR	Cholsey & Wallingford Railway			
DLR	Docklands Light Railway		**NLR**	North London Railway
DMU	Diesel multiple unit		**NSE**	Network South East
ELR	East London Railway (GER, LBSCR, Met, Met Dist & SECR Joint)		**NSWJR**	North & South Western Junction Railway (LNWR, MR & NLR Joint)
EMT	East Midlands Trains		**NXEA**	National Express East Anglia
EMU	Electric multiple unit		**P&P**	'British Railways Past and Present' series (see Bibliography for details)
FCC	First Capital Connect			
FGE	First Great Eastern		**P&PC**	'Past and Present Companion' series (see Bibliography for details)
FGW	First Great Western			
GCR	Great Central Railway		**P&P RR**	'Rediscovering Railways' series (see Bibliography for details)
GER	Great Eastern Railway			
GNR	Great Northern Railway		**RR**	Regional Railways
GWR	Great Western Railway		**SCR**	Swindon & Cricklade Railway
G-WR	Gloucestershire Warwickshire Railway		**SCRP**	Severnside Community Rail Partnership
LBSCR	London, Brighton & South Coast Railway		**SECR**	South Eastern & Chatham Railway
LCDR	London, Chatham & Dover Railway		**SR**	Southern Railway
LM	London Midland		**SWT**	South West Trains
LMSR	London Midland & Scottish Railway		**WA**	West Anglia Railways
LNER	London & North Eastern Railway		**WLR**	West London Railway (GWR & LNWR Joint)
LNWR	London & North Western Railway			
LO	London Overground		**WLER**	West London Extension Railway (GWR, LBSCR, LNWR & LSWR Joint)

Contents

Bibliography

Baker, M. H. C. *British Railways Past & Present No 60: South London Suburban Lines*
    (Past & Present Publishing, 2009; ISBN 978 1 858952628)
Baker, S. K. *Rail Atlas of Great Britain & Ireland*, 12th ed (OPC 2010; ISBN 978 0 86093 632 9)
Bevan, A. *A-Z of Rail Reopenings* (Railway Development Society, 1998; ISBN 0 901283 13 4)
Borley, H. V. *Chronology of London Railways*
    (Railway & Canal History Society, 1982; ISBN 0 901461 33 4)
Brown, J. *London Railway Atlas* (Ian Allan Publishing, 2009; ISBN 978 0 7110 3397 9)
Butt, R. V. J. *The Directory of Railway Stations* (Patrick Stephens Ltd, 1995; ISBN 1 85260 508 1)
Christiansen, R. *A Regional History of the Railways of Great Britain*, Vol 13
    (David & Charles, 1981; ISBN 0 7153 8004 4)
Clinker, C. R. *Great Western Railway – A Register of Halts and Platforms 1903-1979*
    (Avon-Anglia Productions, 1979; ISBN 0 905466 29 2)
Dowling, G. and Whitehouse, J. *British Railways Past & Present*
    No 16: Avon, Cotswolds & The Malverns (Past & Present Publishing, 1993; ISBN 1 85895 077 5)
Gough, T. *Rediscovering Railways: Surrey, East of the County*
    (Past & Present Publishing, 2003; ISBN 1 85895 215 8)
Southern Railway Reflections: The London Area
    (Past & Present Publishing, 2005; ISBN 1 85794 235 3)
Morrison, B. and Brunt, K. British Railways *Past & Present*
    No 7: North East, East and South East London
    (Past & Present Publishing, 1991; ISBN 0 947971 55 6)
    British Railways Past & Present No 13: North West, West and South West London
    (Past & Present Publishing, 1992; ISBN 0 947971 80 7)
Quick, M. *Railway Passenger Stations in Great Britain*
    (Railway & Canal Historical Society, 2009; ISBN 978 0 901461 57 5)
Roose, G. and Ballantyne, H. *British Railways Past & Present No 22: Wiltshire*
    (Past & Present Publishing, 1994; ISBN 1 85895 049 X)
Shannon, P. *British Railways Past & Present*
    No 24: Buckinghamshire, Bedfordshire & West Hertfordshire
    (Past & Present Publishing, 1995; ISBN 1 85895 073 2)
    No 42: Essex and East Hertfordshire (Past & Present Publishing, 2004; ISBN 1 85895 193 3)
Siviter, R. *Past & Present Companion: The Gloucestershire Warwickshire Railway*
    (Past & Present Publishing, 2003; ISBN 1 85895 208 5)
Stretton, M. J. *Past & Present Companion: The Swindon & Cricklade Railway*
    (Past & Present Publishing, 2003; ISBN 1 85895 218 2)
    Past & Present Companion: The Severn Valley Railway
    (Past & Present Publishing, 2010; ISBN 978 1 85794 264 2)
    British Railways Past & Present No 55: Oxfordshire, a Second Selection
    (Past & Present Publishing, 2006; ISBN 1 85895 203 4)
    No 58: North Gloucestershire (Past & Present Publishing, 2008; ISBN 1 85895 257 4)
    No 59: Central Gloucestershire (Past & Present Publishing, 2008; ISBN 1 85895 235 2)
    No 64: South Gloucestershire and Bristol
    (Past & Present Publishing, 2011; ISBN 978 1 85895 269 7)
Waters, L. and Doyle, A. *British Railways Past & Present No 15: Oxfordshire*
    (Past & Present Publishing, 1992; ISBN 0 947971 87 4)

Acknowledgements

Thanks are due to the various people who provided information or otherwise helped in the preparation of this book. These include Nick Catford, Phil Deaves, Mike Franklin, John Hillmer, Roger Marsh, Richard Maund, Colin Pattle, John Stretton and Chris Ward. I am grateful to my wife Cynthia, who waited patiently at Braintree Freeport station while we were on our way from Sherborne to St Petersburg; the result is reproduced on p11. Other diversions were undertaken alone.

Introduction

In the course of preparing this second volume, I was surprised to find that there are so many reopened and indeed new stations or lines in the Greater London area. In addition, every county to the east, immediate north and west also have stations fulfilling the criteria for inclusion. The entries in the following pages range from single-platform stations to grand structures. In the former category is Chafford Hundred, and the latter must surely be St Pancras International and High Speed 1. This volume includes Stratford International, but the remainder of High Speed 1 is covered in Volume 1. Some stations, such as Stevenage, are uninspiring but functional. Others are tastefully designed. The contrast can be extreme – for example, the stations of Melksham and Islip, both managed by the same train operating company until 2011. At the time of writing more new stations are under consideration and I have included some of those most likely to come to fruition, such as Surrey Canal Road. A brand new station for Southend Airport opened in 2011. In contrast, a few stations, mostly opened in the early years following nationalisation of the railways, have since been closed, but they are also included.

New stations have sometimes been built on or close to the site of an earlier one, and I have included data on both the old and new. In many instances the locations have been without a station for decades. Stations are relocated for a variety of reasons, such as a shift of the population centre, better access, or loss of the original site to other developments. Sometimes the original name of the station has been retained and in other instances a new name has been given.

There have been several instances of replacement stations where there was no break in the service. An example is Blackhorse Road, where old was replaced by new on 14 December 1981. I have not included stations in this category unless there was a significant enhancement of facilities.

For the most part, Thameslink uses existing stations and lines. The notable exception to this is the rebuilding of the line through Snow Hill Tunnel and the stations of St Pancras, City Thameslink and Blackfriars. North of the Thames, new Thameslink stations are proposed

at Napsbury, Luton North Parkway, Elstow and Bedford North.

I have not included stations transferred, mostly at the time of nationalisation, to the Underground, examples being Epping and Loughton – in any case, there was usually no break in the passenger service. On the other hand, stations transferred from heavy rail to light rail are covered, including, for example, some stations on the London Tramlink.

In the case of lines, the opening and closing dates refer to use by passenger trains. I have not included new flyovers that have replaced existing level junctions. Thus the flyover between Selhurst and East Croydon is omitted, while the flyover at Stewarts Lane Curve, not duplicating an existing route, is included. Also excluded are new lines parallel to existing lines.

The potential of the North London Line has only been realised in recent years. Prior to that it had almost fallen into a state of dereliction, with several stations closed and those remaining open in a sorry state. The train service was poor and not very reliable. The transformation has been dramatic, with reopened stations and generally clean and smart trains. Part of the closed North London Line that ran to Broad Street has become an extension of the East London Line.

The East London Line, originally a conventional heavy rail line, later became part of Underground. It has now been converted back to heavy rail and is part of London Overground, fully integrated with the capital's railway system. New stations have been built, existing stations refurbished and the line extended.

Construction of the Docklands Light Railway has revitalised long-closed lines, mostly on the North London Line, and given a very good service to communities previously with little. This has been in conjunction with the regeneration of a significant part of the rundown London Docks area for both business and residential purposes.

The West London Line has also seen dramatic changes for the better. Always well used as a cross-London freight route, its passenger potential has been realised in recent years. Kensington Olympia at last has a good passenger service, although it is regrettable that intercity trains only introduced in 1986 no longer use the West London Line. Long-closed stations have been reopened between Willesden Junction and Clapham Junction.

Some lines are used only occasionally by passenger trains, perhaps after many years of freight-only use. They may have opened for a new passenger service, albeit short-lived like Didcot West Curve. Some are short spurs. In such cases it is not always clear when the line first ceased to carry passenger trains, or indeed when they were reinstated. These lines were not always formally closed, although some, such as the Crayford Spur, required legislation in order to run passenger trains again.

There are several schemes worthy of mention, all relating to better rail access to Heathrow. Airtrack was intended to connect the airport with Staines, Woking and the South West, using both open and closed railway routes; it would not have involved any new stations, however, and it was proposed to start services in 2014, but in early 2011 the project was abandoned. There is also discussion on how a high-speed line (referred to as HS 2) from the North of England would feed into a transport hub for the airport. There may also be a station on the Great Western main line from Paddington. Crossrail, although not primarily for the benefit of Heathrow passengers, could form part of the hub; work on it has already started, and it will run from Maidenhead through central London to Shenfield and Abbey Wood. It will result in several existing stations being rebuilt, but no stations in new locations.

Improvements have not been restricted to the London area. Several new stations have opened in Essex and more are planned, for example at Beaulieu Park on the outskirts of Chelmsford. Several new stations have opened in Hertfordshire and there are plans to convert the St Albans Abbey line to a tramway to give a much improved service. Reinstatement of the link between Watford and Croxley Green has been under consideration for many years and may yet come to fruition. The other counties covered by this book have all seen new or reopened stations and lines, with several in Gloucestershire and the Bristol area; more are under discussion, for example on the Portishead branch. Discussions on an east-west rail link north of London have been going on for many years. Several options are under consideration for the eastern end, including a new line between Stevenage and Luton Airport Parkway. In the west, the line already exists and runs from Bletchley to Oxford, the section as far as Bicester currently being for freight only.

Heritage railways feature strongly, ranging from the modest achievements in Oxfordshire and Wiltshire to a 10-mile line from Toddington to Cheltenham. Some of these lines are connected or close to the national network, giving easy access by public transport. As in previous volumes, only those lines where there are at least two operational stations are included.

It has been a very interesting exercise to visit all the locations covered in this book. All the photographs are my own, except where otherwise stated. It has also been encouraging to find that in so many cases it has been the local community that has initiated action.

Using this book

The stations are listed in line order, from Essex to Gloucestershire and the Bristol area. Forest of Dean stations are covered in Volume 3. For each station the name is accompanied by the map reference in Baker's *Rail Atlas of Great Britain & Ireland* (see the Bibliography) – the page number followed by the grid reference. Some stations are not marked in the atlas, in which case the reference is shown in brackets. Then follow the various opening and closing dates, and references, where appropriate, to any other photographs of the location that have been published in Past & Present Publishing's 'British Railways Past & Present', 'Past & Present Companion' and 'Rediscovering Railway' series (again, see the Bibliography). Under 'Operator' are listed the owning company at the Grouping in 1923, and the current organisation managing the station (Train Operating Company or Network Rail), or the operator in the case of a heritage line. Where a station is no longer open, I have entered the name of the operator at closure. For reopened lines, the dates refer to use by passenger trains.

Terry Gough
Sherborne

PLEASE NOTE that details of train services given in this book are correct at the time of writing, but may vary in the future. Always check with the operator before travelling.

Basildon 36, C2

Opened	25 November 1974	The station was built to serve the new town and is situated between Laindon and Pitsea on the Fenchurch Street-Shoeburyness line. It has four trains an hour in each direction, with additional trains during peak periods. There are two trains an hour on Sundays.
Operator original	BR(E)	
current	c2c	

EMUs Nos 357205 (left) and 357218 form down and up services respectively on 13 August 2009.

A down service formed of No 357212 approaches the station on the same day. Note the uneven platform edge. The Class 357s were introduced in 2001.

Chafford Hundred — 36, C2

Opened		30 May 1995
Operator	original	LTS Rail
	current	c2c

This pleasant single-platform station on a loop line serves recently built housing estates and a shopping centre. Trains run daily every half-hour from Fenchurch Street to Southend Central, leaving the main line at Upminster and rejoining it at Pitsea. Most alternate trains continue to Shoeburyness. Additional trains in peak periods terminate at intermediate stations on the loop.

EMU No 357226 leaves the station forming a service to Shoeburyness on 13 August 2009.

Southend Airport — 37, C1

Opened		expected 2011
Operator	original	Stobart Rail
	current	Stobart Rail

The station was due to open on 12 August 2009, but was delayed. The latest date announced was 22 May 2011 but this passed without the station re-opening. It is situated between Rochford and Prittlewell on the Liverpool Street-Southend Victoria line, and is expected to have a half-hourly service.

A visit on the last day of 2010 saw all trains passing through the sation, which was still not open. It is expected to have a half hourly service

Braintree Freeport			37, A1
Opened		8 November 1999	The station, on a branch from the Liverpool Street-Norwich main line, was built primarily to serve the adjacent shopping centre and local housing. Consideration has been given to linking the branch to Stansted Airport with a new line, but this has yet to become a reality.
Operator	original	FGE	
	current	NXEA	

Braintree Freeport station on 5 July 2009.

EMU No 321336 approaches the single platform forming a service from Braintree to Liverpool Street. The service is hourly every day of the week.

Stansted Airport   36, A2

		The station, consisting of a main island platform and a bay, opened at the same time as a new airport terminal building, which is adjacent. It is at the end of a spur from the Liverpool Street-Cambridge line, and trains have access from both the south and north of the main line.
Opened	19 March 1991	
Operator original	WA	
current	NXEA	

Looking toward the junctions with the main line on 4 May 2009, No 317729 is the leading unit on a National Express train from Liverpool Street, from which there is a train every 15 minutes. These trains are branded 'Stansted Express' and have been modified specifically for this service.

National Express also operates an hourly service from Stratford. No 317665 waits in the bay prior to departure.

In the island platform DMU No 170519 forms one of the hourly Cross Country services to Cambridge, the Midlands and the North. On the far right No 317665 leaves with a service to Stratford.

Both faces of the island platform are occupied on 4 May 2009: on the left is No 317654 bound for Liverpool Street, and on the right No 170519.

Stratford International   22, B1

		The platforms are below ground level and the lines emerge from tunnels at each end of the station. The centre island platform is for the Southeastern domestic services and the centre through lines are for Eurostar. The station has no customs and immigration facilities. The platforms on the extreme north and south sides are primarily for the shuttle service that will be run during the Olympic Games in 2012.
Opened	30 November 2009 (preview service); 14 December 2009 (full service)	
Operator original	Network Rail	
current	Network Rail	

On 14 December 2009 an up Eurostar Class 373 rushes through the station on the final leg of its journey from Paris to London.

Access to the Eurostar Depot at Temple Mills is across a viaduct approached from the London end of the station.

An up High Speed Domestic train approaches Stratford on the first day of the full service between London and Kent, 14 December 2009. All these trains are formed of Class 395 electric units, referred to as 'Javelins'.

A St Pancras-Faversham train stops briefly at Stratford.

St Pancras International (Eurostar platforms)	26, B2
Previous name	St Pancras
Opened	1 October 1868
Closed	9 April 2004
Re-opened	14 November 2007
P&P	No 13, pp129, 130
Operator original	MR
current	Network Rail/Eurostar

The stunning refurbished roof of St Pancras station, through which light glistens on the Eurostar trains on clear days, is seen on 29 September 2008

The superb statue of Sir John Betjeman, admiring a line-up of Eurostar trains. The units are Nos 3209, 3206, 3212, 3208 and 3106.

The International platforms are seen here from the buffer stops; there is an unusual lack of passengers, giving the area a rather clinical appearance.

Eurostar passengers (on the right) are segregated from passengers for East Midlands trains (left).

St Pancras International (High Speed Domestic platforms)   26, B2

Previous name	St Pancras	
Opened	12 April 2004 (for Midland Mainline trains)	
Closed	17 July 2006	
Reopened	29 June 2009 (for Southeastern trains)	
P&P	No 13, pp129,130	
Operator **original**	Network Rail	
current	Network Rail/Southeastern	

This is a new station, immediately east of St Pancras MR and adjacent to Eurostar. This part of the terminus was used temporarily by Midland Mainline following closure of the main station in 2004. Thameslink trains from the north also terminated in these platforms during the period that the line between St Pancras and King's Cross Thameslink stations was closed. The full service to Stratford, Ebbsfleet and Ashford International started on 14 December 2009.

Hiding behind copious quantities of glass and metal are two 'Javelin' High Speed Domestic trains on the first day of the full service to Kent, 14 December 2009. On the left is No 395027 and on right No 395026. Further to the left is Eurostar unit No 3218.

A ticket issued on the first day of the full service.

Mid-morning on the first day sees the first unit of the class leaving for Dover. In the background an EMT train leaves for Derby.

On the same day two of the three High Speed Domestic platforms are occupied by trains recently arrived from Dover and Faversham.

St Pancras International (East Midlands platforms)   26, B2

Previous name		St Pancras
Opened		1 October 1868
Closed		9 April 2004
Reopened		17 July 2006
P&P		No 13, pp129, 130
Operator	original	MR
	current	Network Rail/EMT

The new concourse for EMT trains is at the north west end of St Pancras. There are only four platforms, a significant reduction in the space available when St Pancras provided services only to central England.

The East Midlands Trains concourse at St Pancras International on 18 September 2006. The six Eurostar platforms are to the right.

Trains are formed mostly of Class 222 diesel units, known as 'Meridians', built in 2004/05. Typical is the four-car unit approaching St Pancras from Nottingham.

Thameslink

St Pancras International (Thameslink platforms)		26, B2
Opened	9 December 2007	The Thameslink platforms are underneath the main station on the west side. Lack of funding prevented the station from being opened when through Thameslink services were resumed in 2005
P&P	No 13, pp129,130	
Operator original	Network Rail/FCC	
current	Network Rail/FCC	

The glare of headlights sometimes precludes photographing approaching trains in poor light. This is No 319384 about to depart for Brighton on 29 September 2008, despite the rear indicator stating that the train is not in service.

King's Cross Thameslink   26 B2

Previous names:	King's Cross Midland City, King's Cross	This station became a temporary terminus for trains from the south from 11 September 2004 to 15 May 2005 while major construction work was being undertaken around St Pancras.
Opened	1868	
Closed	14 May 1979	
Reopened	11 July 1983	
Closed	9 December 2007	
Operator original	Met	
at closure	FCC	

Electric unit No 319450 enters the confines of King's Cross Thameslink station forming a Brighton line train on 25 September 2006.

City Thameslink — 21, B2

Previous names:	Snow Hill, Holborn Viaduct Low Level (original station), St Paul's Thameslink (present station)
Opened	1 August 1874
Closed	1 June 1916
Reopened	29 May 1990 on new site
Operator original	NSE
current	FCC

This new station is just south of the site of Holborn Viaduct Low Level station and almost underneath the site of the High Level station (closed on 29 January 1990).

This 13 August 2009 view is looking south towards the incline that takes the railway first to ground level, then across Blackfriars Bridge.

Snow Hill Tunnel — 21, B2

Opened	1 January 1866
Closed to passengers	2 April 1916
Closed completely	1969; track lifted 1971
Reopened	16 May 1988
P&P	No 7, pp47, 48; No 60, p45
Operator original	LCDR
current	Network Rail

The Farringdon to Blackfriars line was reinstated with the opening of Snow Hill Tunnel, in preparation for the Thameslink services between Brighton and Bedford, which began a year later. A new section of tunnel at the south end, parallel to the original, was opened in 1990 and the original section closed.

On 16 November 1989 unit No 319038 emerges from the tunnel forming a Bedford-Brighton service, while No 319036 approaches the tunnel with a service to Bedford.

Blackfriars   21, B2

Previous name	St Paul's
Opened	10 May 1886
Closed	see below
P&P	No 7, p49
Operator original	LCDR
current	Network Rail

Blackfriars is situated on the north bank of the River Thames, and is undergoing a major redevelopment. It was both a through station and terminus; the latter (which is to the east of the through platforms) was closed on 22 March 2009. The remaining through platforms have been temporarily extended further on to the bridge over the River Thames while the terminus is being converted for through running to City Thameslink and beyond. It will reopen in late 2012 with longer platforms across the bridge. There will also be a new entrance on the south bank.

On 17 October 1989 electric Class 2EPB (416) unit No 6241 enters Platform 4 with a service from Holborn Viaduct to Dartford. To the right are the terminal platforms.

EMU No 319220 forming a Thameslink service to Sevenoaks approaches the same platform 21 years later.

Trackside and riverside views from 4 May 2010 of the extended temporary platforms Nos 4 and 5 over the River Thames.

Stratford-North Woolwich

Stratford Regional (Low Level)   22, B1

Previous name	Stratford Low Level	This was until 2006 a through station on the North London Line to North Woolwich. It then became a terminus for eastbound trains until they were diverted to new platforms at Stratford High Level. The heavy rail part of Low Level station is currently closed pending conversion for use by DLR trains. These will run from Stratford International to Canning Town and beyond. Jubilee Line Underground trains terminate at adjacent platforms.
Opened	16 October 1854	
Closed	2 January 2009	
Reopened	expected 2011	
P&P	No 7, p37	
Operator original	GER	
current	DLR	

The new station is seen under construction on 26 January 2010

Stratford High Street   (22, B1)

Previous names:	Stratford Bridge, Stratford Market	Although this station closed more than 50 years ago, the main station building at street level in still in good condition and used by a taxi firm and cafes. Part of the building will return to railway use once the platforms are restored for DLR trains.
Opened	14 June 1847	
Closed	6 May 1957	
Reopened	expected 2011	
Operator original	GER	
current	DLR	

The station building is on a bridge, as seen on 16 February 2007. The lines on the left were for North London Line trains and those to the right for Jubilee Line trains. Platforms were beyond the bridge.

By 26 January 2010 construction of the new station is well advanced at both platform level (behind the fencing) and street level. There will be access by steps, ramps and lifts.

West Ham Low Level   22 B1

Opened	14 May 1979
Closed	29 May 1994
Reopened	29 October 1995
Closed	10 December 2006
Reopened	expected 2011
Operator original	BR(E)
current	DLR

The first closure in 1979 was to enable the new Jubilee Line platforms to be built.

In the foreground is the Jubilee Line. The island platform to the right was for North London Line trains and will be used by DLR trains. The High Level station is in the right background in this 16 February 2007 view. (See also page 32.)

Canning Town   22, B1

Previous name	Barking Road
Opened	14 June 1847
Closed and resited	1888
Closed	29 May 1994
Reopened	29 October 1995 close to original site
Closed	9 December 2006
Reopened	expected 2011
Operator original	GER
current	DLR

The station forms part of a transport interchange facility. The High Level platforms are for the DLR line from Poplar to Beckton. The North London line trains used the Low Level island platform to the left, which will be converted for the DLR trains from Stratford. The other Low Level island platform is for Jubilee Line trains.

The DLR High Level platforms are on the right in this 16 February 2007 view. North London line trains used the Low Level island platform to the left, and the other Low Level island platform is for Jubilee Line trains.

Royal Victoria — 22, B2

Previous names:	Tidal Basin, Victoria Dock – Tidal Basin
Opened	1858
Closed	15 August 1943
Reopened	28 March 1994 on new site
Operator original	GER
current	DLR

Unit No 82 is on the rear of a train to Becton on 4 May 2010. The original station was immediately behind the camera. In the present day station in the background is unit No 99 at the front of a four-car train to Tower Gateway. To the left was the double track of the North London Line, which closed in 2009. The track layout has been changed at this point and all that remains is a siding ending at the DLR station.

Custom House — 22 B2

Previous name	Victoria Dock – Custom House	The North London Line will not be converted for use by DLR trains at this station, as there is already an adjacent DLR station. However, it is proposed to reopen the North London Line station as part of Crossrail in 2017.
Opened	26 November 1855	
Closed	28 May 1994	
Reopened	29 October 1995	
Closed	9 December 2006	
Operator original	GER	
on final closure	Silverlink	

On the left of this 16 February 2007 view is the recently abandoned North London Line, parallel to the DLR lines.

Stratford-North Greenwich

Bow Church 22, B1

Previous name	Bow
Opened	26 September 1850
Closed	15 May 1944
Reopened	31 August 1987
Operator original	LNWR/NLR
current	DLR

There is also a DLR line from Stratford High Level, which uses part of the track formation of the former heavy rail line from Victoria Park Junction (Hackney Wick) to North Greenwich. At Bow (and other places listed below) DLR stations have been built on or near the sites of long-closed stations.

Bow Church station on 23 October 2007.

Langdon Park 22, B1

Previous names:	South Bromley, Carmen Street (DLR – not used)
Opened	1 September 1884
Closed	15 May 1944 (last train), 23 April 1945 (formally)
Reopened	10 December 2007 on new site
Operator original	LNWR/NLR
current	DLR

Following the last train, a substitute bus service was provided until formal closure. The present station, which was funded by both central and local government, is a recent addition to this line, and is a short distance (700 yards) south of the long-closed station of South Bromley.

Langdon Park station on 23 October 2007.

All Saints   22, B1

Previous names:	Poplar, Poplar East India Road	Just south of All Saints the DLR deviates from the course of the old line.
Opened	1 August 1866	
Closed	15 May 1944	
Reopened	31 August 1987	
Operator original	LNWR/NLR	
current	DLR	

All Saints station on 23 October 2007.

CrosElement

Crossharbour	22, C1
Previous names:	Millwall Dock, Millwall Docks, Crossharbour & London Arena (DLR)
Opened	18 December 1871
Closed	4 May 1926
Reopened	31 August 1987
Operator original	GER
current	DLR

The DLR picks up the North Greenwich line just north of Crossharbour station. The original station was owned by the Millwall Docks Company, later the Port of London Authority.

Crossharbour station on 23 October 2007.

Island Gardens	22, C1
Previous name	North Greenwich (original site)
Opened	29 July 1872
Closed	4 May 1926
Reopened	31 August 1987
Closed	9 February 1996
Reopened	15 April 1996
Closed	11 January 1999
Reopened	20 November 1999 on new site
Operator original	GER
current	DLR

The first DLR station of this name was built on the site of the terminus of the North Greenwich line, which was on an embankment. The third closure, in 1999, was necessitated by bomb damage. As part of the extension of the DLR to Lewisham, a new Island Gardens station was built below ground and the first station closed. It was subsequently demolished.

In the foreground of this 23 October 2007 view is the new station and in the background is the viaduct on which the old station was located.

West Ham-Fenchurch Street

West Ham High Level — 22, B1

Previous name	West Ham Manor Road
Opened	1 February 1901
Closed	1940; fast platforms abandoned
Reopened	30 May 1999
Operator original	MR (LTSR)
current	LUL& c2c

The station was rebuilt in 1998/99 when the old
Fenchurch Street-Shoeburyness main-line platforms
were reopened after a gap of nearly 60 years.
There was no break in the service provided by
Underground trains, which use separate platforms.

On 16 February 2007 both faces of the main-line island platform are occupied by Class 357 units, with No 357219 on a down service. The Underground platforms are to the right.

Limehouse — 22, B1

Previous names:	Stepney, Stepney East
Opened	6 July 1840 (Blackwall line)
Closed	4 May 1926 (Blackwall line)
Reopened	31 August 1987
Operator original	GER
current	DLR

At Limehouse (then called Stepney), the lines from Fenchurch Street to West Ham (and Shoeburyness) and to Blackwall diverged, the latter being used by the DLR. The West Ham line station has always remained open (apart from temporary closure in 1994 for engineering works).

The Blackwall line at Limehouse (on the right) has been adopted by the DLR.

DLR unit No 24 leaves Limehouse station en route for Bank on 23 October 2007. A train on the Shoeburyness line is in the background.

Blackwall 22 B1

Previous name	Poplar
Opened	6 July 1840
Closed	1845
Reopened	1845 on new site
Closed	4 May 1926
Reopened	28 March 1994 on new site (end-on to previous site)
Operator original	GER
current	DLR

The original Blackwall station was the terminus of the line and closed in 1926. The station currently named Blackwall is on a viaduct adjacent to the sites of the two earlier stations known as Poplar, now under a slip road to an elevated main road (A1261). On the same line was Millwall Junction, the site of which is used by the DLR; it is situated between the present-day stations of Blackwall and Poplar.

The entrance to Blackwall station on 4 May 2010.

Shadwell   22, B1

Previous name	Shadwell & St George's East	There were four tracks from Fenchurch Street, two of which have been given over to the DLR. The remaining two tracks are used by Shoeburyness trains. (See also page 46.)
Opened	1 October 1840	
Closed	22 May 1916	
Reopened	5 May 1919	
Closed	7 July 1941	
Reopened	31 August 1987	
Operator original	GER	
current	DLR	

DLR units Nos 07 and 08 pass the remains of the old up platform, immediately east of the present station, on 23 October 2007.

EMU No 357313, on the parallel Fenchurch Street-Shoeburyness line, passes the new station.

Hackney Wick   22, A1

Previous names:	Victoria Park & Hackney Wick, Victoria Park, Hackney Wick (Victoria Park)
Opened	29 May 1856 (special service)
Closed	30 May 1856
Reopened	14 June 1856 (regular service)
Closed	1 March 1866
Reopened	1 March 1866 on new site
Closed	1 November 1942 (Stratford platform), 8 November 1943 (Poplar platforms)
Reopened	12 May 1980 on second new site
Operator original	LNWR/NLR
current	LO

The new station is situated east of the second earlier station, which was at the junction of the Stratford and Poplar lines. It is on the North London Line and currently has a 15-minute-interval service between Stratford and Richmond.

Right: On 16 February 2007 EMU No 313111 works a North London Line train in Silverlink Metro livery. Responsibility for the trains is now with London Overground, which in 2009 introduced new stock of Class 378.

Below right: Homerton station looking towards Stratford on 16 February 2007.

Homerton   22, A1

Opened	1 October 1868
Closed	15 May 1944 (last train), 23 April 1945 (formally)
Reopened	13 May 1985
Operator original	LNWR/NLR
current	LO

Although the line opened in 1850, a station was not provided at Homerton for a further 18 years. There was a service to Poplar and, from the date of the first opening, also to Stratford. Homerton was closed when the Poplar service was withdrawn, and a substitute bus service was provided until formal closure, a year after the last train ran.

Hackney Central   22, A1

Previous name	Hackney
Opened	1 December 1870
Closed	15 May 1944 (last train), 23 April 1945 (formally)
Reopened	12 May 1980
Operator original	LNWR/NLR
current	LO

As with Homerton, a bus service was provided between the running of the last train and formal closure a year later.

An eastbound service formed by No 313117 leaves the station on 16 February 2007.

Immediately beyond the west end of the station the line is crossed by the line from Liverpool Street to Cheshunt, Stansted Airport and Cambridge (see pages 12, 13 and 40-43).

Dalston Kingsland		21,A2
Previous name	Kingsland	It seems extraordinary that a station should be reopened here after a gap of more than 100 years. Part of the reason is that the original station was replaced by a station named Dalston Junction on the Broad Street branch (see page 50).
Opened	9 November 1850	
Closed	1 November 1865	
Reopened	16 May 1983	
P&P	No 13, p 4	
Operator original	LNWR/NLR	
current	LO	

EMU No 313108 enters the station with a Stratford service on 16 February 2007. Beyond the first bridge and to the left is the site of the line to Broad Street (see below).

This is Western Junction, and beyond here the line is quadrupled. The course of the former line to Broad Street is to the left; this was reinstated following the opening of the extended East London Line from Shoreditch (see pages 47-50).

Kentish Town West   21,A1

Previous name	Kentish Town
Opened	1 April 1867
Closed	18 April 1971 (last train), 20 December 1976 (officially)
Reopened	5 October 1981
Closed	1995/96, for engineering works
Reopened	1996
Operator original	LNWR/NLR
current	LO

This station was closed for the first time due to arson and it was ten years before a new station was built and trains once again stopped here.

The view looking south (towards Stratford) on 16 February 1887.

On the left unit No 313002 heads for Richmond, while the approaching unit, No 313110, is bound for Stratford.

Kilburn High Road 21, B1

Previous names	Kilburn, Kilburn & Maida Vale	This station was also destroyed by fire, hence the 1917 closure. It is situated on the Euston-Watford line and has three trains per hour on weekdays and two per hour on Sundays.
Opened	December 1851	
Closed	1 January 1917	
Reopened	10 July 1922	
Closed	18 September 2004	
Reopened	22 August 2005	
Operator original	LNWR	
current	LO	

There were originally platforms for all six tracks. On the extreme left of this 14 August 2009 view is the main line from Euston, with a Virgin train heading for Birmingham. The lines in the centre are the up and down slow lines, and on the right is the rebuilt station.

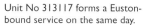

Unit No 313117 forms a Euston-bound service on the same day.

Liverpool Street-Cheshunt

London Fields

22, B1

Opened	27 May 1872	
Closed	22 May 1916	
Reopened	1 July 1919	
Closed	13 November 1981	
Reopened	29 September 1986	
Operator **original**	GER	
current	NXEA	

The second closure was because the station was destroyed by fire. This is the third station out of Liverpool Street and is served by trains to Enfield Town and Cheshunt, both running every 30 minutes, while on Sundays both destinations have hourly trains. Trains to Chingford do not stop here.

EMU No 315849 works a Cheshunt service on 21 August 2007.

A Liverpool Street train consisting of unit No 315843 approaches the station on the same day. There are also lines to the right used by trains to Stansted Airport and Cambridge, which do not stop here.

Graham Road Curve   22, A1
(Reading Lane Junction-Navarino Road Junction)

		This curve was opened for freight traffic only in 1894 and closed to freight in 1965. It first opened for passenger trains following the closure of Broad Street, when North London Line trains were rerouted into Liverpool Street. This service was short-lived and the curve, which is electrified, is not currently used by passenger trains.
Opened	1986	
Closed	1992	
Reopened	9 May 2000	
Closed	29 September 2002	
Operator original	GER	
current	NR	

The double track in the centre is the line between Hackney Central and Kingsland. Navarino Road Junction is in the middle distance, with Graham Road Curve to the left. The view is dated 19 January 2010.

EMU No 315849 passes a steam locomotive as it enters Southbury station forming a Liverpool Street service on 21 August 2007. The engine (No 1016) is in the yard of a builders' merchant; it was built in Finland in 1955, one of 21 'Pacifics' of Class Hr1 used by Finnish State Railways, and was shipped to England in 1990.

Southbury   26, B1

Previous name	Churchbury
Opened	1 October 1891
Closed	1 October 1909
Reopened	1 March 1915
Closed	1 July 1919
Reopened	21 November 1960
Operator original	GER
current	NXEA

The original main station building survived the closures and was returned to railway use when the station reopened in 1960.

Turkey Street	26, B1
Previous name	Forty Hill
Opened	1 October 1891
Closed	1 October 1909
Reopened	1 March 1915
Closed	1 July 1919
Reopened	21 November 1960
Operator original	GER
current	NXEA

None of the original buildings survive and Turkey Street is a basic station with a simple waiting shelter on each platform.

No 315842 enters the station with a Cheshunt service on 21 August 2007. There is a ticket machine and kiosk at the ground-level entrance.

The Cheshunt-bound platform at Turkey Street.

Theobalds Grove   26, A1

Opened	1 October 1891
Closed	1 October 1909
Reopened	1 March 1915
Closed	1 July 1919
Reopened	21 November 1960
Operator original	GER
current	NXEA

This is the first station on the line outside Greater London.

On 21 August 2007 unit No 315842 arrives from Cheshunt, where the service to Liverpool Street starts. The only reminder at platform level of an earlier station here is the old brick wall.

At ground level, the original building has been retained, with the addition of a small entrance porch.

New Cross Gate-Dalston Junction (East London Line)

Surrey Canal Road   (22, C1)

Opened	13 March 1871 (line only)
Closed	1913
Reopened	expected 2012 (line only – no date for station)
Operator original	ELR
current	none

There is much local pressure for a new station to be built on the southern extension of the East London Line, which will run from Surrey Quays to the South London Line between South Bermondsey and Queens Road Peckham. The station is unlikely to open at the same time as the line because of insufficient funding.

This is the proposed site of the station on 27 January 2010, with Millwall football stadium to the left, several nearby factory units and housing behind the camera. The footpath follows the alignment of the old railway line. In the background, on an embankment, is the London Bridge-East Croydon line.

Surrey Quays   22, C1

Previous names:	Deptford Road, Surrey Docks
Opened	7 December 1869
Closed	25 March 1995
Reopened	25 March 1998
Closed	23 December 2007
Reopened	27 April 2010 (preview service), 23 May 2010 (full service)
Operator original	ELR
current	LO

Until recently the East London Line was part of the Underground, and trains ran only from Shoreditch to Surrey Quays, then either to New Cross or New Cross Gate. The line has been rebuilt and now connects with the rest of the London heavy rail network, the trains being operated by London Overground. A preview service between New Cross Gate and Dalston Junction was due to start on 15 April 2010, but was postponed at the last minute until 27 April. Trains ran every 8 minutes, increased to every 5 minutes when the full service was introduced.

Surrey Quays station under reconstruction on 27 January 2010.

Rotherhithe		22, B1
Opened	7 December 1869	Just beyond Rotherhithe station the line passes under the River Thames.
Closed	25 March 1995	
Reopened	25 March 1998	
Closed	23 December 2007	
Reopened	27 April 2010 (preview service), 23 May 2010 (full service)	
Operator original	ELR	
current	LO	

EMU No 378153, seen here on 4 May 2010, was one of several units operating the preview service between New Cross/New Cross Gate and Dalston Junction.

Wapping	22, B1
Previous name	Wapping & Shadwell
Opened	7 December 1869
Closed	23 March 1995
Reopened	23 March 1998
Closed	23 December 2007
Reopened	27 April 2010 (preview service), 23 May 2010 (full service)
Operator original	ELR
current	LO

This is the first station on the north bank of the Thames. It is a cramped station with narrow platforms on a curve, and there is a feeling of being compressed against the wall as trains approach.

No 378136 stands in the northbound (Dalston Junction) platform on 4 May 2010.

Shadwell · 22, B1

Previous name	Shadwell & St George's-in-the-East
Opened	10 April 1876
Closed	23 March 1995
Reopened	23 March 1998
Closed	23 December 2007
Reopened	27 April 2010 (preview service), 23 May 2010 (full service)
Operator original	ELR
current	LO

The ELR station is at right angles to the DLR station of the same name, which is at a higher level (see page 34)

With such a frequent service, trains pass at most stations, as here on 4 May 2010.

Whitechapel · 22, B1

Proposed name for original station:	De Beauvoir Town (not used)
Opened	10 April 1876
Closed	23 March 1995
Reopened	23 March 1998
Closed	23 December 2007
Reopened	27 April 2010 (preview service), 23 May 2010 (full service)
Operator original	ELR
current	LO

For many years trains from New Cross and New Cross Gate terminated here, the service only continuing to Shoreditch during the rush hour and on Sunday mornings. All trains now continue northward, although Shoreditch has been closed.

Unit No 378154, which worked the first passenger train on the rebuilt line, heads for New Cross Gate on 4 May 2010.

No 378137 works a New Cross Gate to Dalston Junction service at Whitechapel. The District and Hammersmith & City Lines station of the Underground is at a higher level and at right-angles to the East London Line station, and the lines are carried on the bridge seen in the background. There will be an interchange here with Crossrail.

Shoreditch High Street		21, B2
Opened	27 April 2010 (preview service), 23 May 2010 (full service)	This is a new station on the site of Bishopsgate Goods Yard. It is a through station, replacing the nearby terminus of Shoreditch, and, although on a viaduct, is enclosed in a huge concrete box. Train announcements were made by staff with megaphones during the preview period.
Operator original	LO	
current	LO	

The station is enclosed in a huge concrete box.

The ground-level entrance to Shoreditch High Street station is uninspiring, but inside the station there is a spacious ticket hall and wide staircases to the platforms. The viaduct in the background is of historic significance and carried sidings that formed part of Bishopsgate Goods Yard.

Hoxton   21, B2

Opened	27 April 2010 (preview service), 23 May 2010 (full service)	The line from the new Shoreditch High Street station picks up the formation of the line from Broad Street to Dalston Junction, past the site of a long-closed station (also named Shoreditch) to the new station of Hoxton.
Operator original	LO	
current	LO	

The new Hoxton station on 19 January 2010.

There are some short but steep inclines on the line, typified by the approach to Hoxton. Unit No 378151 descends into the station on 4 May 2010.

Haggerston		21, B2
Opened	2 September 1867	The new station is on the same site as the original.
Closed	6 May 1940	
Reopened	27 April 2010 (preview service), 23 May 2010 (full service)	
Operator original	NLR/LNWR	
current	LO	

Unit No 378142 approaches the summit of the climb from Dalston Junction as it enters Haggerston station on 4 May 2010.

Dalston Junction   21, A2

Opened	1 November 1865
Closed	30 June 1986
Reopened	27 April 2010 (preview service), 23 May 2010 (full service), 22 February 2011 (through platforms)
P&P	No 7, p4
Operator original	LNWR/NLR
current	LO

The new Dalston Junction is on the site of the original station and is currently the northern terminus for some East London Line trains. The connection to the present North London Line at Dalston Western Junction (see page 37) was made in 2011. The two centre platforms are terminal and on both sides are the through platforms for the trains that continue to Highbury & Islington. The station is above ground on an enclosed concrete raft above which business premises are being built.

This is the view from the end of the platform on 4 May 2010, as unit No 378154 enters the station.

The terminal platforms are occupied by Nos 378142 (right) and 378146. All stations and trains on the line were spotlessly clean at the time of the author's visits during the preview period. It is to be hoped that they remain so, once passenger numbers increase.

South Acton Junction-Old Kew Junction   20, C2

Opened	1 June 1854
Closed to passenger trains	1940
Reopened to passenger trains	26 September 1999
Closed to passenger trains	29 September 2002
Operator original	NSWJR
current	Network Rail

It was not until 1999 that the line was reopened for regular passenger trains, for a new service running between Basingstoke and Chelmsford. It was named 'Crosslink' but was short-lived, partly because journey times were regarded as excessively long and it therefore attracted fewer than anticipated passengers. There were six trains each way on weekdays and five on Sundays.

On 25 March 1962 a special train touring little-used South London lines behind Class 'O2' No 30199 is seen at South Acton. The line to Old and New Kew Junction continues to the right, while the line to the left is used today by the frequent trains running between Stratford, Willesden Junction and Richmond.

Willesden Junction-Clapham Junction

Mitre Bridge Curve (Willesden High Level Junction-Mitre Bridge Junction)   20, B2

Opened	2 September 1867
Closed to passenger trains	3 October 1940
Reopened to passenger trains	25 September 1994
Operator original	LNWR
current	Network Rail

Willesden Junction High Level station consists of an island platform. Just to the south of the station is Willesden High Level Junction where the lines to Richmond and Clapham Junction diverge; the Clapham Junction line turns east to take the Mitre Bridge Curve.

Unit No 313103 is heading for Richmond with a service from Stratford on 13 August 2009. It will join the line from Kew (see above) at South Acton Junction. In the background is Willesden High Level Junction signal box, which closed on 27 February 2011. The viaduct on the right carries trains to Stratford into the other face of the platform. Clapham Junction trains, which use Mitre Bridge Curve to reach Willesden High Level, also run to Stratford, but do not call at all intermediate stations.

Mitre Bridge Curve is on an embankment for much of the way and access is limited. Unit No 313107 negotiates the curve on a Stratford service.

In the foreground is Mitre Bridge Junction; the line to the right is from Willesden High Level and to the left from Willesden main line (West London Junction). Unit No 313120 crosses Mitre Bridge on a service to Clapham Junction. The bridge spans the Grand Union Canal and the main line from Paddington. Current collection changes from overhead to third rail just beyond Mitre Bridge.

West London Junction-Mitre Bridge Junction　　20, B2

Opened	27 May 1844	This curve was virtually out of use by passenger trains by 1940; some through trains continued after this date, but not on a regular basis. It was not until the introduction of Intercity trains from south of the Thames to the Midlands and North that a regular service was reintroduced. Recent changes have resulted in these trains no longer running, but instead there is an hourly service between East Croydon and Milton Keynes.
Closed	1940	
Reopened	12 May 1986 (for Intercity trains)	
Operator original	LNWR	
current	Network Rail	

EMU No 350124 approaches West London Junction with a Milton Keynes service on 13 August 2009. This curve is also used by several freight trains a day. The site of Willesden Junction Main Line station (closed 3 December 1962) is behind the camera.

A train from Milton Keynes to East Croydon formed of unit No 350125 approaches Mitre Bridge Junction.

Shepherds Bush		20, B2
Previous name	Uxbridge Road	
Opened	1 November 1869	
Closed	21 October 1940 (due to enemy action)	
Reopened	28 September 2008	
Operator	**original**	WLR
	current	LO

A ticket issued on the first weekday of reopening.

For about a year Cross Country ran a service from the North to the South Coast via Kensington Olympia and Clapham Junction, having taken over from Virgin Trains. This Class 220 unit is on the daily Manchester Piccadilly-Brighton service on 29 September 2008.

On the first day of the full service at Shepherds Bush, EMU No 313116 works a Stratford-Clapham Junction service. The train on the left, heading towards Willesden, consists of unit No 377211 on an East Croydon-Milton Keynes service.

Kensington (Olympia)   21, C1

Previous names:	Kensington, Kensington Addison Road
Opened	2 June 1862
Closed	21 October 1940 (due to enemy action)
Reopened	19 December 1946 (for District Line and unadvertised main-line trains)
Closed	11 June 1956
Reopened	1 April 1963 (Euston rebuilding)
Closed	15 June 1965
Reopened	24 May 1966 (Motorail terminal only); 15 October 1967 (Paddington resignalling)
Closed	20 December 1967 (except unadvertised Clapham Junction trains and Motorail)
Reopened	5 May 1969 (for advertised Clapham Junction trains); 12 May 1986 (for regular Intercity services)
Closed	1988 (Motorail terminal only)
P&P	No 13, pp32-33
Operator original	WLR
current	LO

An infrequent shuttle service known as the 'Kenny Belle' from Clapham Junction started in 1946, primarily for postal workers. It was sometimes shown in the public timetables in the early 1950s, then omitted until 1969 when a footnote warned that times were subject to alteration at short notice. The service consisted of two morning trains from Clapham Junction to Kensington Olympia (no public return service) and two evening trains in the opposite direction, again with no return service. It was finally shown as operating in both directions until the service ceased in 1994. Class 2MT No 84022 has just arrived with the afternoon shuttle from Clapham Junction on 22 March 1961.

Top and above: A frequent service between Clapham Junction and Willesden Junction began in 1994 and was operated by diesel units, such as No L702 seen on 21 July 1994.

Sister unit No L700 forms a Willesden Junction to Clapham Junction service. By this time the third rail had been laid in preparation for electrification. On the left is the site of the Motorail Terminal, from which trains ran to several places including Fishguard, Perth and St Austell.

Class 47 No 47830 approaches the station with a Brighton to Manchester Piccadilly service on 21 July 1994. These services ceased in December 2008.

Freight trains pass frequently through the station – here a Class 60 diesel locomotive hauls a train of hoppers on the northbound through line on 26 September 2004. Underground trains from Earls Court only ran during exhibition days, and the bay to the right was opened specifically for such services in 1958. A frequent daily service began in 1988 and currently runs from High Street Kensington.

West Brompton		21, C1
Opened	1 September 1866	
Closed	21 October 1940 (due to enemy action)	
Reopened	30 May 1999	
Operator	original	WLER
	current	LO

A Virgin Cross Country Class 220 unit passes through the station forming a Manchester Piccadilly-Brighton service on 28 July 2004. The large buildings in the background are part of the Earls Court Exhibition Centre.

In addition to the frequent passenger train service, there are freight trains to be accommodated. The platforms for the Underground (District Line) are to the left and the line follows the retaining wall before descending into a short tunnel under the Network Rail line. The District Line station has never closed, although there was a Monday-to-Friday-only service for many years.

Imperial Wharf	21, C1
Previous names:	Chelsea, Chelsea & Fulham; proposed name for new station: Chelsea Harbour (not used)
Opened	2 March 1863
Closed	21 October 1940 (due to enemy action)
Reopened	28 September 2009 on new site
Operator original	WLER
current	LO

Construction of this station should have started before this photograph was taken on 17 November 2004. EMU No 313102 passes the site.

The station was opened in 2009, and is seen here on 14 December. It was built on a new site, although there had been a station about half a mile to the north. This is the newest station on the line and was funded by Transport for London, St George plc and two local councils. Unit No 313112 heads for Clapham Junction.

Latchmere Junctions	21, C1
Previous name	Latchmere South Western Junction
Opened	2 March 1863
Closed to passenger trains	21 October 1940
Reopened	See below
Operator original	WLER
current	Network Rail

There are three junctions close together here, as seen on 24 September 2004. Looking towards Kensington, in the distance is Junction No 2 and slightly nearer is Junction No 1. To the right is the Sheepcote Lane Curve from Junction No 3. The nearest station was Battersea (500 yards west), which closed on 21 October 1940. A local Member of Parliament is pressing for the station to be reopened.

Latchmere Junction No 2-Ludgate Junction	21, C1
Opened	1863
Closed to passenger trains	21 October 1940
Reopened	5 May 1969
Operator original	WLER
current	Network Rail

The curve connecting Latchmere and Ludgate junctions is on a viaduct. All manner of odd rolling stock was used on the Kensington-Clapham Junction trains until electrification, and on 5 June 1989 an electro-diesel locomotive was used with a 4TC unit, in this instance No 8007. After this turn, the unit was regularly used on a late-afternoon Waterloo-Bournemouth service. The curve is currently used by Stratford trains.

DMU No 117724 works a Willesden Junction-Clapham Junction service on 21 February 1996,
during the final year before electrification.

The same unit has just passed Ludgate Junction (to the left beyond the rear of the train).
From Ludgate Junction, trains use the former LSWR lines to access the north side of Clapham Junction.

Latchmere Junction No 1-Falcon Junction   21, C1

		This line passes under the lines from both Waterloo and Victoria to reach the south side of Clapham Junction, and was the route taken by Intercity trains to the South Coast. The curve is currently used by the East Croydon-Milton Keynes trains.
Previous name	Latchmere Main Junction-Clapham South Junction	
Opened	2 March 1863	
Closed to passenger trains	21 October 1940	
Reopened	5 May 1969; 12 May 1986 (to Intercity trains)	
P&P	No 60, p34	
Operator original	WLER	
current	Network Rail	

Class 'H' No 31542 brings a Kensington Olympia-Clapham Junction train up the gradient to Clapham Junction on 11 July 1962. In the background is a suburban train from Victoria.

Latchmere Junction No 3-Factory Junctions (a,b and c)   21, C1

		Passenger services were withdrawn on 15 December 2008, but a new service began on 18 May 2009, with one train per day between Wandsworth Road and Kensington Olympia on Mondays to Fridays only, not stopping at intermediate stations. This was expected to be extended to Ealing Broadway from May 2010, but this did not materialise.
Opened	2 March 1863 (Latchmere Junction-Longhedge Junction); 3 April 1866 (Longhedge Junction-Factory Junction)	
Closed	1 October 1917	
Reopened	12 May 1986 (for Intercity trains)	
Operator original	WLER and SECR	
current	Network Rail	

On 2 August 1991 diesel locomotive No 56031 works one of the many freight trains on this line. It has just passed under the main lines from Waterloo and Victoria, a little to the east of Clapham Junction. It will pass under the Victoria line twice more before reaching Factory Junction. The electrified lines on the left are from the north side of Clapham Junction.

The approach to Factory Junctions 'c' and 'b' is on a viaduct. On 28 August 1991 an Intercity train from Liverpool Lime Street to Dover Western Docks, hauled by No 47842, is held on the viaduct as empty stock (Class 4EPB No 5434) heads for Stewarts Lane Depot. The platform in the foreground is one of two at Wandsworth Road, for use by South London Line trains between London Bridge and Victoria. These trains take the first ('a') of the Factory Junctions and reach Victoria via Battersea Park.

Sheepcote Lane Curve (Latchmere Junction No 3-West London Junction)   21, C1

Opened	6 July 1865
Closed	13 March 1912 (to passenger trains), 21 January 1936 (completely)
Track removed	1937
Reopened	29 May 1994
Closed	25 May 2004 (to trains), 14 December 2004 (replacement bus service withdrawn)
Operator original	WLER
current	Network Rail

This curve was used by empty Eurostar trains travelling between Waterloo and the Eurostar Depot at North Pole Junction, as well as by regular but infrequent passenger trains. The latter were replaced by a bus service running between Waterloo and Kensington Olympia, which ran on Tuesdays only in the early hours of the morning and was to satisfy legal requirements prior to formal closure of the curve. The curve is currently out of use to all traffic.

This is the curve on 23 Sept 2004 looking from the West London Junction end, with Latchmere Junction No 3 in the background.

A Eurostar train has just passed over West London Junction on its way to Waterloo International on the same day.

The 'Night Riviera' sleeper service was run from Penzance to Waterloo via Kensington Olympia from 1995 to 1998, when it was transferred to Paddington. This is the empty stock with diesel locomotive No 47811 on the rear, passing through Queens Road station on 31 May 1996. Just beyond the bridge, which carries the Victoria-Clapham Junction lines, is West London Junction. Eurostar trains used the line on the far right.

Stewarts Lane Curve (Linford Street Junction-Nine Elms Junction)   21 C1

Opened	14 November 1994	This curve was built exclusively for Eurostar trains to provide a link between the terminus at Waterloo International and the former SECR line from Victoria to Kent. Although not formally closed, it is not currently in use.
Closed	13 November 2007	
Operator original	Railtrack	
current	Network Rail	

Construction of the viaduct at Stewarts Lane on 28 August 1991.

The site of the new Linford Street Junction on the same day. Class 411 (4CEP) EMU No 1616 passes with a Victoria-Maidstone East service.

This is the viaduct trackbed looking towards Nine Elms Junction. At right-angles are the former LSWR lines from Waterloo. The low-level lines are from Victoria to Stewarts Lane Depot and Clapham Junction, the latter used only by empty stock and special passenger trains.

A Eurostar train descends from the viaduct to Nine Elms Junction and on to Waterloo on 17 June 1996. The electric unit in NSE livery is on the former LSWR main line.

Waterloo ('Windsor' side)   21, B2

Previous names:	Waterloo 'North Station', 'Windsor Lines', Waterloo International	This entry refers to the 'Windsor' side of Waterloo, which was rebuilt with four platforms to accommodate Eurostar trains. This part of the station is currently out of use, but there are proposals to reopen it to relieve pressure on the main station.
Opened	3 August 1860; additional 'North' platforms 1885	
Closed	June 1990	
Reopened	14 November 1994	
Closed	13 November 2007	
Reopened	2014?	
P&P	No 13, pp42-43	
Operator **original**	LSWR	
current	Network Rail	

A line-up of three Eurostar trains in Waterloo International on 2 February 1995, from left to right Nos 3204, 3209 and 3231.

Unit No 3209 at the buffer stops, waiting to depart on a train to Brussels.

Left: The lower concourse and entrance to the Eurostar platforms.

Below: The impressive roof of the Eurostar station is seen from Platform 19 of the main station. Power car No 43029 is at the head of an Intercity train to Cardiff via Kensington – this train of seven coaches had just one passenger. To the right is the main station with suburban unit No 5915 of Class 455 forming a Windsor service on 2 February 1995.

A final view of the impressive Eurostar station during its short life, but now deserted in favour of St Pancras. The date is 20 June 2002.

Ticket issued three days after commencement of Eurostar services.

The leaflet was given to all passengers on boarding the train.

Wimbledon-West Croydon

Merton Park — 17, B1

		A shuttle service consisting of two-car electric units ran between Wimbledon and West Croydon for decades, but became increasingly run-down and the decision was taken to convert much of the line to a light railway, extending to East Croydon and beyond. Tram stops were provided at or near all the original stations and several new stops added.
Previous name	Lower Merton	
Opened	1 October 1868	
Closed	1 June 1997	
Reopened	30 May 2000	
Operator original	LBSCR/LSWR	
current	London Tramlink	

Tramlink unit No 2534 stops at Merton Park, a former junction station and the first stop from Wimbledon. This 30 October 2007 view is looking from the divergence of the two lines; the abandoned line curving to the left to Merton Abbey is now a footpath.

This is the view looking towards Wimbledon, before which there is now an additional stop.

Morden Road | 17, B1

		This former single-platform halt now has a passing loop and two platforms, in a rather cramped location adjacent to a main road overbridge.
Opened	March 1857 (first appearance in timetable)	
Closed	1 June 1997	
Reopened	30 May 2000	
P&P	No 60, p96	
Operator original	LBSCR	
current	London Tramlink	

Trams run every few minutes to New Addington. This is the station on 30 October 2007.

Mitcham | 17, B1

		There is virtually no trace of the original station here.
Previous names:	Morden, Morden Halt, Morden Road Halt	
Opened	22 October 1855	
Closed	1 June 1997	
Reopened	30 May 2000	
P&P	RR Surrey (East), p17	
Operator original	LBSCR	
current	London Tramlink	

Trams operated for several months prior to opening to the public, and one such run is seen at Mitcham being operated by unit No 2531 on 12 October 1999.

Beddington Lane
17, B2

Previous names:	Beddington, Beddington Lane Halt
Opened	22 October 1855
Closed	May 1997
Reopened	30 May 2000
P&P	RR Surrey (East), p14
Operator original	LBSCR
current	London Tramlink

This was another single-platform halt, now benefitting from a passing loop with a platform on each side.

No 2534 approaches forming a Wimbledon service on 30 October 2007.

Waddon Marsh
17, B2

Previous names:	Waddon Marsh Halt
Opened	6 July 1930
Closed	1 June 1997
Reopened	30 May 2000 on new site
P&P	RR Surrey (East), pp11-13; P&P No 60, pp92-95
Operator original	SR
current	London Tramlink

Waddon Marsh Halt was a simple island platform, used mainly by workers at the nearby factories. There were sidings serving the adjacent gas works and power station, and it is still an industrial area, which the trams serve well. The tram stop is a little further toward West Croydon than was the halt.

Trams Nos 2545 and 2543 approach each other on 10 September 1999, during the test period.

Clapham Junction/Tulse Hill-Mitcham Junction

Mitcham Eastfields 17, B1

		This station, on a new site, has staggered platforms on either side of a level crossing.
Opened	2 June 2008	
Operator original	Southern	
current	Southern	

On 30 October 2007 EMU No 456019 passes the site of the station at speed during construction, forming a service from Victoria to Epsom.

The station has two trains an hour between St Albans and Wimbledon. Victoria-Epsom trains are half-hourly; in this instance unit No 455809 forms an up train on 11 September 2008.

London Bridge-Sanderstead

New Beckenham-Beckenham Junction Curve 18, A1

Opened	1857	The curve was singled in 1987 and the remnant of the down line used for stabling stock. It was a further eight years before passengers trains began to use this line again. It is currently used only at peak times, for trains running between Charing Cross and Beckenham Junction.
Closed to passenger trains	30 September 1935	
Reopened	26 May 1995 (legislation date)	
Operator original	SECR	
current	Network Rail	

EMU No 465019 is about to pass the curve with a Hayes-Cannon Street service on 3 September 2009.

Woodside 18, B1

Previous names:	Woodside & South Norwood	Woodside is served by circular tram routes Nos 1 and 2, which both run from Croydon, the former to Elmers End and the latter to Beckenham Junction. All that remains of the original station here are the steps to the old up platform and the main building at street level, part of which is currently used by a taxi firm.
Opened	July 1871	
Closed	1 June 1997	
Reopened	23 May 2000	
Operator original	SECR˘	
current	London Tramlink	

Tram No 2535 heads for Elmers End on 30 October 2007.

Addiscombe		17, B2
Previous names:	Bingham Road, Bingham Road Halt	The original station was on an embankment, which was removed in preparation for street-level tram lines.
Proposed original names	Addiscombe Park (not used)	
Opened	1 September 1906	
Closed	15 March 1915	
Reopened	30 September 1935	
Closed	16 May 1983	
Reopened	23 May 2000	
P&P	No 60, p75	
Operator original	SECR	
current	London Tramlink	

On 30 October 2007 tram No 2530 has just left the station to cross a road, immediately beyond which was the old station.

On the same day a tram from Beckenham Junction waits in the station for the crossing lights to change before proceeding to East Croydon. The headboard erroneously displays West Croydon, which was not accessible because of road works.

Dartford Loop

Crayford Spur (Crayford Spur A junction to B junction)   38, C1

Opened	1918	This spur is situated between Slade Green and Crayford and until recent years was used only for empty stock workings to Slade Green Depot. It currently has a half-hourly service on Mondays to Fridays, an hourly service on Satudays and no service on Sundays. Trains do circular trips, starting and finishing at Cannon Street by way of Hither Green, Slade Green and Deptford, and vice versa. There is also a curve connecting Barnehurst with Slade Green, which is used by empty stock and a limited number of passenger trains. It has never been closed/reopened as far as can be ascertained.
Closed	1920	
Reopened	11 October 1942	
Closed	prior to 1963	
Reopened	1 April 1998	
P&P	No 60, p75	
Operator original	SECR	
current	Network Rail	

EMU unit No 465030 enters the curve at Junction B on 3 September 2009. The line in the foreground is for Dartford.

Unit No 465040 rounds the curve on an anticlockwise service on the same day.

Eltham | 22, C2

Opened	17 March 1985	This new station replaced Eltham Well Hall and Eltham Park, and was built in conjunction with a new road scheme and bus interchange. There are four trains an hour to Dartford, with alternate trains from Victoria and Charing Cross. Some additional rush-hour trains continue to Gillingham. On Sundays, only the Charing Cross trains run.
Operator original	BR(S)	
current	Southeastern	

Eltham station on 30 October 2007.

Heathrow

Stockley Park Flyover (Heathrow Tunnel Junction-Heathrow Airport Junction) 19, C1

Opened	19 January 1998	The flyover was built to enable the frequent trains from Heathrow to join the main route to Paddington without conflicting with main-line trains.
P&P	No 60, p75	
Operator original	Railtrack	
current	Network Rail	

On the flyover on 29 September 2008 is a Class 332 'Heathrow Express' electric unit. On the left are the up and down slow lines and on the right the fast lines for Reading and further west.

Heathrow Junction   19, C1

Opened	19 January 1998
Closed	25 May 1998
Operator original	Railtrack
on closure	Railtrack

This was a temporary station necessitated by the collapse of part of the tunnel into Heathrow Airport, just prior to inauguration of the new services from Paddington. It was located on a spur just before the tunnel mouth, a location chosen because it was clear of the main line and adjacent to a major road leading to the airport.

Electric locomotive No 90147 is on a test train in the station in January 1998 prior to opening. Shuttle buses to the airport ran from the left-hand side of the platform. Construction work on the tunnel can be seen on the right. *Chris Ward*

This view is looking in the opposite direction on 9 January 2009. The spur to the temporary station ran from just beyond the containers and between the two fences to terminate adjacent to the tunnel portal, which is immediately behind the camera. A 'Heathrow Connect' train, consisting of unit No 360204, has just emerged from the tunnel.

Heathrow Terminals 1,2 and 3   19, C1

Previous names:	Heathrow Central (Underground services)	This station serves the three older terminals clustered round the central part of Heathrow Airport. It is served by both 'Heathrow Express' and 'Heathrow Connect' services.
Opened	22 May 1998 (Paddington services)	
Operator original	Heathrow Express	
current	Heathrow Express	

A 'Heathrow Express' train on 7 October 2008.

Heathrow Terminal 4   19, C1

Opened	25 May 1998 (Paddington services)	This is the terminal station for the Heathrow Connect services, which call at five intermediate stations on the main line, with an overall journey time of 37 minutes. The first train of the day (on weekdays) leaves Paddington shortly before 05.00 and the last train leaves just before midnight; trains run every half-hour between these times. The service begins later on Sundays and is hourly. 'Heathrow Connect' services are expected to be withdrawn once Crossrail reaches Heathrow, the current estimate being 2017.
Operator original	Heathrow Express	
current	Heathrow Express	

Unit No 360201 has recently arrived from Paddington on 7 October 2008.

Heathrow Terminal 5   19, C1

Opened	27 March 2008	Only 'Heathrow Express' serves Terminal 5, and the trains run every 15 minutes from 05.00 to midnight every day of the week. They stop only at the station for Terminals 1, 2 and 3 and are then non-stop to Paddington. The total journey time is 21 minutes.
Operator original	Heathrow Express	
current	Heathrow Express	

Two views of Heathrow Terminal 5 on 7 October 2008.

Colnbrook Estate Halt (19, C1)

Previous names:	Colnbrook Estate
Opened	1 May 1961
Closed	29 March 1965
Operator original	BR(W)
on closure	BR(W)

This was a single-platform halt for the benefit of workers at this Buckinghamshire industrial estate. It was a request stop, with a train approximately every hour, including Sundays. A separate station a quarter of a mile to the south, served the village of Colnbrook. The line is still open for freight traffic and continues to the Bath Road in Colnbrook.

Seen on 7 September 2009, the halt was on the west side of the line, approximately adjacent to the second large building on the left, which was built after the halt closed.

Poyle Estate Halt (19, C1)

Previous names:	Poyle Estate
Opened	4 January 1954
Closed	29 March 1965
Operator original	BR(W)
on closure	BR(W)

Formerly in Middlesex, now Buckinghamshire, this was a simple structure with a waiting shelter. It was a mandatory stop for peak-hour trains and a request stop for the remainder of the day. The entrance to the station from the adjacent industrial estate is still in use and gives access to a footpath along the trackbed. There was a proposal (now withdrawn) to use the southern end of the branch for a new line from Staines West Curve to Heathrow Terminal 5, which would turn east a short distance before the site of the halt.

Poyle Estate Halt in about 1960. *Nick Catford*

HERTFORDSHIRE
Stevenage area

Welham Green

36, B1

Opened	29 September 1986
P&P	No 42, p114
Operator original	NSE
current	FCC

This new station was funded by BR and the local and county councils. It is on the edge of an industrial estate and close to modern housing estates. Platforms are only provided on the up and down slow lines; the centre lines are used by expresses from King's Cross to the North of England and semi-fast trains to Cambridge and Peterborough.

EMU No 313041 is on the rear of a train from Welwyn Garden City to Moorgate on 4 May 2009. This service is provided three times an hour on Mondays to Fridays, while at weekends there are two trains an hour, which use King's Cross instead of Moorgate.

The leading unit of this train from Cambridge to King's Cross is No 365506.

Watton-at-Stone   36, B1

Opened	2 June 1924	This station is on a secondary line that connects with the main line from King's Cross to the north at Alexandra Palace and Stevenage. It was reopened with funding from local councils, the county council and BR after campaigning by local residents. There is an hourly service (half-hourly during peak periods) between Moorgate and Letchworth Garden City. At weekends trains use King's Cross instead of Moorgate and only run as far as Stevenage.
Closed	11 September 1939	
Reopened	17 May 1982	
Operator original	LNER	
current	FCC	

Services at Watton-at-Stone are provided by Class 313 electric units, as Nos 313026 seen in the upper picture and No 313045 in the lower one, photographed on 4 May 2009.

Stevenage   36, A1

Opened	7 August 1850
Closed	23 July 1973
Reopened	23 July 1973 on new site
Operator original	GNR
current	FCC

The new station, with significantly enhanced facilities, is situated about 1½ miles south of the original station in order to better serve the New Town.

On the afternoon of 4 May 2009 a service to King's Cross formed of unit No 313043 sets off from Stevenage for Langley Junction, where it will take the line to Watton-at-Stone.

Unit No 365535 uses the up fast line on the half-hourly service from Peterborough to King's Cross. This calls at all intermediate stations north of Stevenage and will run fast to Finsbury Park. Alternate trains call at all stations throughout the journey.

There is an hourly semi-fast service between Cambridge and King's Cross worked by Class 365 units, in this instance No 365537. There are also trains between these two points that run hourly and call at all stations.

Not all trains at Stevenage are electrically powered. Diesel power car No 43310 is on the rear of a King's Cross to Edinburgh express on 4 May 2007.

Arlesley   35, A2

Previous names:	Arlesey Siding, Three Counties
Opened	1 April 1866
Closed	5 January 1959
Reopened	1 October 1988
Operator original	GNR
current	FCC

Arlesey is on the East Coast Main Line, served by trains from Peterborough to King's Cross. There was a station named Arlesey & Henlow 1½ miles to the north, which opened in 1850, but this also closed on 5 January 1959.

On the left unit No 365535 forms a service to Peterborough on 4 May 2009, while on the through line driving van trailer No 82207 rushes toward King's Cross on a train from Newcastle.

The service is hourly on Mondays to Fridays (more at peak periods) and Sundays, yet there are two trains per hour on Saturdays. Unit No 365531 enters the station forming an (almost) all-stations service to King's Cross.

St Albans Abbey branch

How Wood 24, A1

Opened	24 October 1988	A shuttle service is provided by electric trains operating between Watford Junction and St Albans Abbey. There is a train every three-quarters of an hour on weekdays and one an hour on Sundays. The station was built primarily to serve the residents of new housing estates and was funded by local councils. It is in a pleasant location giving access to country walks. There is a plan to convert the line into a tramway, in order to provide a much more frequent service at a reasonable cost, with the possibility of extending the service into the town centres at St Albans and Watford. The scheme is backed by central and local government and it is hoped to begin the tram service in 2012. This branch is supported by ALCRP.
Operator original	NSE	
current	LM	

EMU No 321428 operates a late morning shuttle on 3 April 2009.

Garston   23, A2

Opened	7 February 1966
Operator original	BR(M)
current	LM

The station at Garston is also adjacent to new housing. It is well used, particularly by commuters and schoolchildren. It appears as 'Garston (Hertfordshire)' in current timetables, which seems odd as the station of the same name on Merseyside closed in 2006

Only one unit is required to operate the service; on 3 April 2009 No 321428 is seen again.

Watford-Croxley Green

Watford Stadium   23, B2

Opened	4 December 1982
Out of use by	14 May 1993
Closed	22 March 1996
Operator original	BR(M)
on closure	NSE

The building of this station was funded by football organisations and the local council. It did not appear in public timetables and was used only by football excursion trains. It is on the Watford High Street to Croxley Green line, which has for years been the subject of campaigns supported by local authorities for its reopening. It is not planned to reopen Watford Stadium station, but Watford West would be reopened and there would be a new station at Ascot Road to replace Croxley Green. The earliest reopening date for the line is 2014.

The remains of Watford Stadium station on 3 April 2009.

BEDFORDSHIRE

Luton Airport Parkway 35, B2

		The station, which has platforms for the fast and slow lines, is close to the M1 motorway and linked to the airport by a dedicated bus service. It is used by EMT and FCC trains.
Opened	21 November 1999	
Operator original	Thameslink	
current	FCC	

On 3 April 2009 a St Pancras-Nottingham train is formed of four-coach 'Meridian' unit No 222009. There is a half-hourly service to various towns in the East Midlands.

To the right a train from Nottingham is formed of unit No 222007 *City of Derby*, while on the extreme left is unit No 377203 on a Bedford-Brighton service.

Bedford St Johns   43, C2

Previous names:	Bedford, Bedford St Johns Halt
Opened	18 November 1846
Closed	1 August 1862
Reopened	1 August 1862 on new site
Closed	14 May 1984
Reopened	14 May 1984 on second new site
P&P	No 24, pp35-36
Operator original	LNWR
current	LM

The previous station was on the Bedford-Cambridge line, and when this closed the station became a terminus for trains from Bletchley. The station was later relocated less than half a mile to the north-west on a freight-only line to enable Bletchley trains to reach Bedford's main-line station. The new station was funded in part by the county council, and an hourly service is currently provided on Monday-Saturday only; there is no Sunday service. The line is promoted by MVCRP.

Bedford St Johns station on 3 May 2009.

BUCKINGHAMSHIRE
For Staines West branch see page 81

Milton Keynes Central   35, A1

Opened	14 May 1982
Operator original	BR(M)
current	LM

The station is an integral part of the new town and was funded by the development corporation and BR. It has three island platforms, one with a bay, giving a total of seven platform faces. It is used by long-distance trains from Euston to the Midlands and the North, and there are typically six trains an hour in each direction. It is also the northern terminus for trains on the hourly service from East Croydon.

The uninspiring design of the station buildings is made worse by the visual intrusion of overhead electricity equipment for the trains. These views are looking towards Euston on Sunday 3 May 2009, when there were very few trains because of engineering works. As a result the platforms are uncharacteristically deserted.

A lone train eventually appeared, but this was an empty stock working in the form of unit No 350118.

An array of station nameboards serves as ample reminder of the location.

Aylesbury Vale Parkway 35, B1

Opened	14 December 2008
Operator original	CR
current	CR

This entry includes the reopening of the line from Aylesbury, which had been closed to regular passenger trains since 5 September 1966. The station was not due to open until 2010, but opened early. It is situated about 3 miles north-west of Aylesbury and close to the A41 trunk road. There is an hourly service from Marylebone every day of the week, with additional trains during peak hours.

The official opening date for the station was on 3 July 2009, but it was in use several months prior to this. On 8 May DMU No 165017 arrives at the incomplete station forming a service from Marylebone.

In May 2009 there was still work to be done in completing the buildings, forecourt and car park.

This overall view of the station shows unit No 165022 approaching from the south-east and a gigantic storm coming in from the north-west. The line to the left leads to Quainton Road, where there is a working steam museum known as the Buckinghamshire Railway Centre.

Haddenham & Thame Parkway   35, B1

Previous names:	Haddenham	This station was reopened with a single platform, a mile south of the original station. A second platform was added when the line was doubled a decade later. Funding was provided by central government and two county councils.
Opened	2 April 1906	
Closed	7 January 1963	
Reopened	5 October 1987 on new site	
Operator original	GWR/GCR	
current	CR	

There are half-hourly services between Marylebone and Birmingham Snow Hill, as well as from Marylebone to Bicester North; some trains continue to Stratford-upon-Avon. On 8 May 2009 a London-bound train from Bicester North is in the hands of diesel unit No 165020.

The late-morning service to Stratford-upon-Avon on the same day is worked by No 165025.

Water Eaton Parkway   34, B2

Previous names:	Oxford Road Halt
Opened	9 October 1905
Closed	1 January 1917
Reopened	5 May 1919
Closed	25 October 1926
Reopened	expected 2013
P&P	No 13, pp42-43
Operator original	LNWR
on opening	CR

This station will be on the Bicester Town line between Oxford and Islip. It will be adjacent to an existing park & ride facility for Oxford and on the site of Oxford Road Halt.

Light engine No 66019 passes the site of the station on 13 October 2010, which is currently used as a stone distribution depot.

Islip   34, B2

Opened	1 October 1850
Closed	1 January 1968
Reopened	15 May 1989
P&P	No 15, p85; No 55, pp48-49
Operator original	LNWR
current	CR (from 22 May 2011)

This is currently the only intermediate station on the reopened line from Oxford to Bicester, recently named the 'Bicester Link', and was reopened two years after the line. The well-maintained station, which has a single platform, is located in pleasant surroundings on the edge of the village. There are five morning trains, then a gap of about 3 hours, followed by six more trains, with an extra late-night train on Fridays. There are nine trains on Sundays.

Left and opposite top: Islip station, photographed on 3 May 2009.

Bicester Town   34, B2

		The rebuilding of this station (and that at Islip) was funded by local councils. Passenger trains terminate here, but the line continues to Bletchley. A chord will be built at Bicester to connect with the Marylebone line south of Bicester North station, and is expected to open before the end of 2013. There is also strong support to reopen the line to Bletchley as part of an east-west link.
Previous names:	Bicester, Bicester London Road	
Opened	1 October 1850	
Closed	1 January 1968	
Reopened	11 May 1987	
P&P	No 55, pp45-46	
Operator original	LNWR	
current	CR (from 22 May 2011)	

The station originally had two platforms and the remains of the abandoned platform can be seen on the right in this 3 May 2009 view. The line continues over the level crossing to Bletchley.

Wallingford — 34, C2

Opened	2 July 1866
Closed	15 June 1959; occasional special trains thereafter
Reopened	17 June 1967
Closed	23 June 1968; occasional special trains thereafter
Reopened	April 1988 on new site, but no regular service until 1999
P&P	No 15, pp26-27; No 55, p124
Operator original	GWR
current	CWR

The station lies at the end of the branch from Cholsey, on the main line between Reading and Didcot. The present station is very close to the site of the original station, which was demolished in 1969. This is a heritage line and services are provided on weekends in the spring and summer, with six trains in each direction.

Wallingford station on 8 May 2009.

Didcot West Curve (Didcot West Curve Junction to Foxhall Junction) 34, B2

Opened	15 February 1886	The regular passenger service operated between Bristol Temple Meads and Oxford, and there were typically nine trains per day each way, with one originating from Bicester Town and some going beyond Bristol.
Closed	no record found	
Reopened	16 May 1988 to passenger trains, 27 September 1999 to regular passenger trains	
Closed	28 September 2002 to regular passenger trains, 18 May 2003 to all passenger trains	
Operator original	GWR	
current	Network Rail	

Foxhall Junction on 27 June 2009.

WILTSHIRE

Hayes Knoll   33, C2

Opened	2000
P&PC	SCR, pp116-119, 123
Operator original	SCR
current	SCR

The Swindon & Cricklade Railway is another heritage line, and uses part of the MSWJR trackbed just north of Swindon. Train services run at weekends for most of the year with a half-hourly service. There are additional trains on Bank Holidays and Wednesdays during school holidays.

Hayes Knoll station on 15 June 2003. *John Stretton*

Blunsdon station on 13 January 2009. *John Stretton*

Below right: Black Dog Halt on 19 May 1956. *Norman Simmons, Photos of the Fifties*

Blunsdon   33, C2

Opened	1 September 1894
Closed	28 September 1924
Reopened	1983 (rides only), 1999 to Hayes Knoll
P&PC	SCR, pp64-66, 110-115, 120-125
Operator original	MSWJR
current	SCR

This is the southern terminus of the line, although the company intends to extend to Mouldon Hill. Track has been laid part of the way and preparatory work continues towards Mouldon Hill.

Black Dog Halt   (33, C2)

Previous names:	Black Dog Siding	The station was 4 miles south-east of Chippenham on the Calne branch; no mileage was shown against the station in the public timetable until about 1960. In the 1950s there were up to 15 trains per day on the branch, and two on Sundays. In the 1960s this rose to 20 per day and seven on Sundays, and some had 1st Class accommodation. The halt remained a request stop throughout its existence.
Opened	3 November 1918 (private station), 15 September 1952 (to the public)	
Closed	20 September 1965	
P&P	No 22, pp42-44	
Operator original	GWR	
on closure	BR(W)	

Hawkeridge Curve (Hawkeridge Junction to Westbury East Loop Junction)   9,A1

		The Hawkeridge Curve, north-east of Westbury, opened for regular passenger trains on 22 May 2011. A new Bristol Temple Meads-Paddington service was introduced, the morning train going via Westbury, but the evening return train avoids Westbury by using the Hawkeridge Curve. The Curve has been used by freight trains and occasionally as a diversionary route for passenger trains for many years and more recently on one day per week by the Penzance sleeper, but this is the first time it has been used on a daily scheduled basis, as far as can be ascertained.
Opened	14 July 1942	
Closed	never formally closed	
P&P	No 22, pp60-61	
Operator original	GWR	
current	Network Rail	

In the foreground is the Bath-Westbury line, and leading to the right is the Hawkeridge Curve, seen on 9 December 2010.

Melksham   9,A1

Opened	5 September 1848
Closed	18 April 1966
Reopened	13 May 1985
P&P	No 22, p49
Operator original	GWR
current	FGW

Melksham station on 28 April 2009.

Melksham is between Chippenham and Trowbridge, and prior to closure there were 14 trains per day in each direction on weekdays and six on Sundays; many ran between Paddington and Westbury. The line remained open during the period that the station was closed, but was singled, and the present station occupies the site of the old down platform. There is currently a Monday-Friday service of one train in the early morning from Gloucester and one in the evening from Worcester Foregate Street, both running to Southampton Central. On Saturdays there are two trains, and on Sundays one, and the pattern is similar in the other direction. There is a campaign to improve the service, but this is unlikely to happen in the near future because of the severe shortage of rolling stock and additional costs involved. However, if plans for new services from Westbury to Oxford and Salisbury to Swindon come to fruition, Melksham will have an improved service.

GLOUCESTERSHIRE
Branches from Kemble

Chesterton Lane Halt 33, B2

Opened	2 February 1959	Lightweight railbuses were introduced on the Cirencester and Tetbury branches on 2 February 1959 and several halts opened or reopened. Chesterton Lane Halt, consisting of a rail-level platform of sleepers, was located three-quarters of a mile before the end of the branch at Cirencester Town. Prior to this there were no intermediate stations on the branch.
Closed	6 April 1964	
Operator original	BR(W)	
on closure	BR(W)	

The rudimentary Chesterton Lane Halt in about 1959. *John Stretton*

Park Leaze Halt (33, B2)

Opened	4 January 1960	This halt was 2½ miles from Cirencester Town, and 1½ miles from Kemble, and was the only other intermediate station on the line. There were up to 17 trains per day each way, and all stopped at both stations. On Sundays four trains each way called at the halts. All trains were 2nd Class only.
Closed	6 April 1964	
Operator original	BR(W)	
on closure	BR(W)	

The site of Park Leaze Halt on 18 August 2009.

Church's Hill Halt (33, C2)

Opened	2 February 1959
Closed	6 April 1964
Operator original	BR(W)
on closure	BR(W)

This halt was on the Tetbury branch, almost 4 miles from Kemble. It too had a good service, with a train about every hour. There was, however, no Sunday service.

Church's Hill Halt in about 1959. *John Stretton*

Trouble House Halt (33, C2)

Opened	2 February 1959
Closed	6 April 1964
Operator original	BR(W)
on closure	BR(W)

This was a basic sleeper-built platform on the Tetbury branch, 5 miles from Kemble, and serving the public house of the same name.

Trouble House Halt in about 1959. *John Stretton*

Culkerton Halt   33, C2

Previous names:	Culkerton, Culkerton May	This was the only proper station on the Tetbury branch, downgraded to a halt on reopening. Prior to its first closure there was a weekday service of seven trains, then on reopening this was increased to nine. There was no Sunday service and all trains were 3rd/2nd Class.
Opened	2 December 1889	
Closed	5 March 1956	
Reopened	2 February 1959	
Closed	6 April 1964	
P&P	No 59, pp105-106	
Operator original	GWR	
on closure	BR(W)	

Culkerton Halt in about 1959. *John Stretton*

Jackament's Bridge Halt   (33, C2)

Opened	3 July 1939
Closed	27 September 1948
Reopened	1959, unofficially in use
Closed	1964, with closure of line
Operator original	GWR
current	BR(W)

This halt was between Kemble and Culkerton. All trains called here until the first closure; the station was never officially reopened, but when the railbuses were introduced they did call if requested.

The remains of the entrance to Jackament's Bridge Halt which was on the embankment. This is the view on 16 August 2009.

Toddington 33, A2

Opened	1 December 1904	Prior to first closure most trains ran between Honeybourne and Cheltenham Spa. There were typically eight trains each way per day on weekdays only. The present-day heritage line now has up to six trains per day to Cheltenham Racecourse. Toddington is currently at the north-east end of the line, but it will not remain a terminus for many more years, as construction of an extension to Broadway is well advanced. The line as far as Laverton reopened on 2 April 2011, but passengers are not permitted to disembark. Toddington is an attractively presented station with good facilities both operationally and for the travelling public. The railway's locomotive shed and works are located here.
Closed	7 March 1960	
Reopened	22 April 1984 (trains ran for about 700 yards), 8 March 1987 (service to Winchcombe)	
P&P	No 16, p61; No 58, pp102-105; P&PC G-WR, pp86-88	
Operator original	GWR	
current	G-WR	

An impressive signal gantry guards access to the station, which can be seen in the background. Beyond the station is the line towards Broadway.

A general view of Toddington on 9 April 2009, revealing that it has been renovated to represent a typical GWR station.

A view of the station looking towards Cheltenham.

A closer view shows the attention to detail that recreates the atmosphere of a steam-era station.

Winchcombe		33, A2
Opened	1 February 1905	The station has been reconstructed, as much was demolished following closure. The main building came from Monmouth Troy, but the end result is a station that looks as though it was here from the original opening just over 100 years ago.
Closed	7 March 1960	
Reopened	8 March 1987	
P&P	No 58, pp97-99; P&PC G-WR, pp91-92	
Operator original	GWR	
current	G-WR	

A view of the station looking towards Cheltenham on 9 April 2009.

Class '5600' No 5619 approaches the station on a train to Cheltenham.

Winchcombe is the headquarters of the railway's Carriage & Wagon Department.

Looking back towards Toddington, on the far end of the platform is the signal box, which came from Hall Green, Birmingham. Just beyond this is the Carriage & Wagon works, for which the former goods shed is used.

Gotherington Halt   33, A2

Previous names:	Gotherington	The station currently in use was constructed specifically for the reopened line and consists of a single short platform with waiting shelter.
Opened	1 June 1906	
Closed	13 June 1955	
Reopened	summer 2003	
P&P	No 58, pp93-94; P&PC G-WR, p97	
Operator original	GWR	
current	G-WR	

The original station (on the left) has been restored, but is a private house, as seen on 9 April 2009.

A typical GWR halt and associated railway items now occupy the former goods yard, which is also privately owned.

Only a small number of trains stop here, mostly mid-week.

Cheltenham Racecourse 33, A2

Opened	13 March 1912	Following closure of the line, the track was lifted, but relaying reached here at the end of 2000. It was another three years before trains ran into Racecourse station, initially specials, then regular passenger trains. The road-level booking office is the original, but the building on the platform is new.
Closed	25 March 1968	
Reopened	16 March 1971 for occasional special trains	
Closed	18 March 1976 (last passenger train), 1 November 1976 (completely)	
Reopened	12 April 2003 (first public train)	
P&P	No 58, pp88-90; P&PC G-WR, p99	
Operator original	GWR	
current	G-WR	

GWR Class '5600' No 5619 enters the station on a morning service from Toddington on 9 April 2009.

The signal box is new, built to the same design as that at Gotherington Halt and modelled on a typical GWR example.

Ashchurch for Tewkesbury — 33, A2

Previous names:	Ashchurch; proposed new name: Tewkesbury Parkway
Opened	24 June 1840
Closed	15 November 1971
Reopened	1 June 1997
P&P	No 16, p53; No 58, pp5, 63-72
Operator original	MR
current	FGW

This one-time junction station now consists of basic up and down platforms, connected by a footbridge. It serves nearby industrial and business parks and local housing, as well as being the railhead for Tewkesbury, hence the proposal to rename it, which is under discussion between the local supporters and First Great Western. It is served approximately hourly by trains from Great Malvern and Worcester Shrub Hill to Gloucester and Bristol Temple Meads. Some trains continue to, for example, Weston-super-Mare or Weymouth. On Sundays there are four trains each way.

No 43301 rushes through the station heading a service from Edinburgh to Plymouth on 16 August 2009. The single track to the right is the remnant of the line to Evesham, which now leads only to a nearby MOD vehicle depot. There was also a line to the left, which went to Tewkesbury and Great Malvern, now under the station car park. The water tower in the left background is almost the only remaining building linked with the past.

DMU No 150239 works the first train of the day, a Worcester Shrub Hill to Weston-super-Mare service.

Gloucester Over Junction 33, B2

Opened	8 February 1990	This was a temporary station by the River Severn at Over, built to assist passengers unable to reach Gloucester due to flood damage to the railway bridge. It was adjacent to the A40 trunk road, enabling a rail replacement bus to provide a service to the city. The site is still recognisable from the base of Over Junction signal box and the remnants of the access road.
Closed	circa 21 February 1990	
Operator original	Railtrack	
on closure	Railtrack	

Diesel unit No C396 operates a service to Cardiff, its home base, on 17 February 1990. *David McCollum*

Another view of the temporary station. *David McCollum*

Cam & Dursley 33, B1

Previous names:	Dursley Junction, Coaley Junction, Coaley	This park & ride station is 150 yards east of the site of the former Coaley station; the latter was situated in the vee of the junction for the Dursley branch, which closed to passengers in 1962. The new station is the result of pressure from local residents, who eventually won the support of the county council and other official bodies. Work on the new station, which was funded by county and local councils, and the Rural Development Commission, began in the autumn of 1993.
Opened	17 September 1856	
Closed	4 January 1965	
Reopened	29 May 1994 on new site	
P&P	No 59, p58	
Operator original	MR	
current	FGW	

DMU No 158766 departs with a Weymouth-Gloucester service on 30 March 2009.

The old station was just this side of the first road bridge. An express from Penzance heads for Birmingham New Street past the site of the old station.

The functional station forecourt. The bus shelter is on the extreme left, and the car park is behind the camera.

Diesel locomotive No 66301 heads south on a freight train on 30 March 2009.

Yate		33, C1
Opened	8 July 1844	On weekdays Cam & Dursley and Yate are served hourly by the same trains, which operate between Gloucester, Bristol Temple Meads and stations beyond. There are four trains on Sundays (more during the summer months).
Closed	4 January 1965	
Reopened	15 May 1989	
P&P	No 16, p89; No 59, p66	
Operator original	MR	
current	FGW	

The platforms at Yate are staggered, and seen through the intervening road bridge is unit No 150246 forming a train to Westbury on 30 March 2009. The building on the extreme right is the old goods shed, now in use for other purposes.

An express from Derby heads for Plymouth. On the left is the line to Tytherington Stone Terminal, part of the branch to Thornbury, which closed to passengers in 1944.

This Plymouth-Derby train consists of two 'Voyager' units on 30 March 2009. To the right is one of several factories in close proximity to the station, and there is also plenty of housing in the area.

A car park is provided for commuters to Bristol and other passengers.

BRISTOL AREA

Bristol Parkway   28,B2

		The station is located at Stoke Gifford on the Paddington-South Wales main line and close to several motorways. A new station was built on the same site in 2001. It has three platforms that are surprisingly narrow and can get very crowded. There are plans to add a fourth platform
Opened	1 May 1972	
Opened	1 July 2001	
Operator original	BR(W)	
current	FGW	

In this view from 17 October 2008 the down main-line platform is on the extreme left; the left-hand face of the island platform is for up trains and the right face is usually used for trains terminating or originating here. Diesel unit No 158763 will work one of the services to Cardiff Central, which run every half-hour.

Trains arrive and depart every few minutes for much of the day, with services to London, the Midlands, South Wales, Bristol, the West and South West. On 21 September 2009 one of the hourly Paddington-Swansea trains is seen on the left and in the centre a Penzance-Birmingham train. On the extreme right railbus No 143618 works a local service to Weston-super-Mare.

A general view of the station and yards. The freight train, hauled by No 66221, will leave immediately after the London-bound express in the foreground has cleared the section. In the down platform is a Swansea train, and in the loop a train from Weston-super-Mare.

An overall view of the station and car park.

Filton Abbey Wood | 28, B2

		The present station was built for the Ministry of Defence and replaced Filton Junction. It is also close to the Airbus factory and the University of the West of England. Stations in the Bristol area are promoted by SCRP.
Previous names:	Filton, Filton Junction	
Opened	8 September 1863	
Closed	4 October 1886	
Reopened	4 October 1886 on new site	
Closed	11 May 1910	
Reopened	11 May 1910 on second new site	
Closed	11 March 1996	
Reopened	11 March 1996 on third new site	
Rebuilt with extra platform	2004	
P&P	No 16, p106	
Operator original	GWR	
current	FGW	

This general view of the station shows DMU No 150239 on a service from Weston-super-Mare to Bristol Parkway. The MOD Procurement Agency establishment is to the right beyond the trees, while in the opposite direction is housing. The platform on the extreme left, added in 2004, is for trains to South Wales; the line through this platform is also used by freight trains to Hallen Marsh Junction and Avonmouth (see page 124).

There is step-free access to all three platforms, on which are located simple waiting shelters. There is a booking kiosk, but this not open on a regular basis.

Express trains frequently pass through the station, such as these running from Bristol Temple Meads to Derby and to Birmingham New Street on 27 June 2009.

Unit No 150121 *Silver Star*, recently transferred from Silverlink Metro, operates a morning service from Weston-super-Mare to Cardiff Central at Filton Abbey Ward.

Below: Photographed on 29 June 2009, the line under the bridge at Feeder Bridge Junction is the up main line from Bristol Temple Meads to Paddington. The lines curving to the right lead to Dr Day's Bridge Junction and Filton Abbey Wood.

Bristol Avoiding Line (Dr Day's Bridge Junction-Feeder Bridge Junction)   28, C2

Other names:	Bristol Loop, Rhubarb Loop Curve	Only one passenger train per day has used this line in recent years, namely the 13.38 from Westbury to Bristol Parkway. However, from May 2011 a new service was introduced from Bristol Parkway to Bath with one late-afternoon train taking the Bristol loop.
Opened	29 May 1886	
Closed	prior to 1979 to passenger trains (probably not formally closed)	
Reopened	29 May 1994 to passenger trains	
Operator original	GWR	
current	FGW	

Chiltening Platform   (28,A1)

Previous names:	Chittening Factory Platform
Opened	5 March 1917
Closed	11 October 1923
Reopened	27 October 1941 (unadvertised)
Closed	1 August 1946
Reopened	25 August 1947 (workmen only), 31 May 1948 (to public)
Closed	23 November 1964
Operator original	GWR
current	BR(W)

All that remains at Chittening is the eastbound platform, seen here on 10 June 2009.

The station was built for workers at the local factories and was characterised by having a very long waiting shelter on each platform. In the years leading up to closure there were two morning and two evening trains between Bristol Temple Meads and Avonmouth Dock, while on Sundays there was just one train, which ran mid-afternoon. There are large industrial estates in the vicinity, but no plans to reopen the station. The line is still open for freight traffic from Filton Junction/Patchway Junction/Bristol Parkway to Hallen Marsh Junction and Avonmouth on the Severn Beach branch.

Ashton Gate Halt   (28,C2)

Previous names:	Ashton Gate Platform	**Closed**	1977
Opened	15 September 1906	**Reopened**	12 May 1984
Closed	1917	**Closed**	19 May 1984
Reopened	23 May 1926	**Operator original**	GWR
Closed	7 September 1964	**current**	BR(W)
Reopened	29 September 1970 (used intermittently)		

There are conflicting dates in the various literature sources for some of the opening and closing dates. The station was used occasionally by special trains (mostly for football events) even when it was closed to regular passenger trains. Prior to the second closure, there was an hourly service between Bristol Temple Meads and Portishead on weekdays and five trains on Sundays. The station was used only for football specials during its third opening. The football ground has recently been sold to a supermarket chain for redevelopment, and the site for the proposed new stadium is half a mile further from the station. There is a local campaign to reopen the station, the proposal being to use Ashton Gate as the terminus for trains from Severn Beach, which currently terminate at Bristol Temple Meads. The reopening of the whole line to Portishead (North Somerset) is also under consideration by the relevant councils, FGW and Network Rail. The line continues to be used intermittently for freight traffic, in recent years only as far as Portbury Docks.

The two abandoned platforms at Ashton Gate, devoid of all buildings, seen here on 10 June 2009.

Bitton		9, A1
Opened	4 August 1869	Prior to closure a train service was provided between Bristol Temple Meads and Bath approximately hourly on weekdays only. The station, now in South Gloucestershire, has been well restored by the AVR, with additional buildings including a buffet. The current service is operated by both diesel and steam traction, and there are five or six trains per day at weekends and on some weekdays between spring and autumn; fewer trains run in the winter months. The Avon Walkway between Bristol and Bath runs alongside the line.
Closed	7 March 1966	
Reopened	1999 (for trains to Oldland Common)	
Operator original	MR	
current	AVR	

The Avon Valley Railway's Bitton station on 3 June 2009.

Oldland Common 9, A1

Previous name	Oldland Halt	This station is also part of the heritage Avon Valley Railway.
Opened	2 December 1935	
Closed	7 March 1966	
Reopened	1999	
Operator original	LMSR	
current	AVR	

A further view of the Avon Valley Railway's Bitton station on 3 June 2009.

In the platform at Oldland Common on 3 June 2009 are diesel vehicles Nos 52006 and 52025 of Class 107, both originally allocated to Scotland. No 52025 became a Sandite vehicle on withdrawal from passenger use. Both have previously been used on other heritage lines and arrived on the AVR in September 2008.

Avon Riverside (Somerset)		9, A1
Opened	11 May 2004	This new station is close to the Avon Valley Country Park. There is a picnic area and boat trips can be taken. A long-term aim of the railway is to extend the line to Newbridge, on the outskirts of Bath.
Operator original	AVR	
current	AVR	

The AVR's Avon Riverside station on 3 June 2009.

Index of locations